1

**CONVENTION BETWEEN
THE GOVERNMENT OF THE UNITED STATES OF AMERICA
AND THE GOVERNMENT OF THE KINGDOM OF BELGIUM
FOR THE AVOIDANCE OF DOUBLE TAXATION AND THE
PREVENTION OF FISCAL EVASION
WITH RESPECT TO TAXES ON INCOME**

The Government of the United States of America and the Government of the Kingdom of

Belgium, desiring to conclude a Convention for the avoidance of double taxation and the

prevention of fiscal evasion with respect to taxes on income, have agreed as follows:

## Article 1

### GENERAL SCOPE

1. This Convention shall apply only to persons who are residents of one or both of the Contracting States, except as otherwise provided in the Convention.

2. Except as provided in subparagraph a) of paragraph 4 of Article 22 (Relief from Double Taxation), the Convention shall not restrict in any manner any benefit now or hereafter accorded:

  a) by the laws of either Contracting State; or

  b) by any other agreement to which the Contracting States are party.

3. a) Notwithstanding the provisions of sub-paragraph b) of paragraph 2 of this Article:

    i) for purposes of paragraph 3 of Article XXII (Consultation) of the General Agreement on Trade in Services, the Contracting States agree that any question arising as to the interpretation or application of this Convention and, in particular, whether a taxation measure is within the scope of this Convention, shall be determined exclusively in accordance with the provisions of Article 24 (Mutual Agreement Procedure) of this Convention; and

    ii) the provisions of Article XVII of the General Agreement on Trade in Services shall not apply to a taxation measure unless the competent authorities agree that the measure is not within the scope of Article 23 (Non-Discrimination) of this Convention.

  b) For the purposes of this paragraph, a "measure" is a law, regulation, rule, procedure, decision, administrative action, or any similar provision or action.

4. Except to the extent provided in paragraph 5, this Convention shall not affect the taxation by a Contracting State of its residents (as determined under Article 4 (Resident)) and its citizens.  Notwithstanding the other provisions of this Convention, a former citizen or former long-term resident of a Contracting State may, for the period of ten years following the loss of such status, be taxed in accordance with the laws of that Contracting State.

5. The provisions of paragraph 4 shall not affect:

a)      the benefits conferred by a Contracting State under paragraph 2 of Article 9 (Associated Enterprises), paragraphs 1 b), 2, 5, 6 and 9 of Article 17 (Pensions, Social Security, Annuities, Alimony, and Child Support), and Articles 22 (Relief from Double Taxation), 23 (Non-Discrimination), and 24 (Mutual Agreement Procedure); and

b)      the benefits conferred by a Contracting State under paragraph 7 of Article 17 (Pensions, Social Security, Annuities, Alimony, and Child Support), Articles 18 (Government Service), 19 (Students, Trainees, Teachers and Researchers), and 27 (Members of Diplomatic Missions and Consular Posts), upon individuals who are neither citizens of, nor have been admitted for permanent residence in, that State.

6.      An item of income, profit or gain derived through an entity that is fiscally transparent under the laws of either Contracting State shall be considered to be derived by a resident of a State to the extent that the item is treated for purposes of the taxation law of such Contracting State as the income, profit or gain of a resident.

## Article 2

### TAXES COVERED

1.      This Convention shall apply to taxes on income imposed on behalf of a Contracting State irrespective of the manner in which they are levied.

2.      There shall be regarded as taxes on income all taxes imposed on total income, or on elements of income, including taxes on gains from the alienation of property.

3.      The existing taxes to which this Convention shall apply are:

a)      in the case of Belgium:

i)      the individual income tax;

ii)      the corporate income tax;

iii)      the income tax on legal entities; and

iv)      the income tax on non-residents;

including the prepayments and the surcharges on these taxes and prepayments;

b)      in the case of the United States:

    i)    the Federal income taxes imposed by the Internal Revenue Code (but excluding social security taxes); and

    ii)    the Federal excise taxes imposed with respect to private foundations.

4.    The Convention shall apply also to any identical or substantially similar taxes that are imposed after the date of signature of the Convention in addition to, or in place of, the existing taxes. The competent authorities of the Contracting States shall notify each other of any changes that have been made in their respective taxation or other laws that significantly affect their obligations under this Convention.

## Article 3
## GENERAL DEFINITIONS

1.    For the purposes of this Convention, unless the context otherwise requires:

    a)    the term "person" includes an individual, an estate, a trust, a partnership, a company, and any other body of persons;

    b)    the term "company" means any body corporate or any entity that is treated as a body corporate for tax purposes according to the laws of the state in which it is organized;

    c)    the terms "enterprise of a Contracting State" and "enterprise of the other Contracting State" mean respectively an enterprise carried on by a resident of a Contracting State, and an enterprise carried on by a resident of the other Contracting State; the terms also include an enterprise carried on by a resident of a Contracting State through an entity that is treated as fiscally transparent in that Contracting State;

    d)    the term "enterprise" applies to the carrying on of any business;

    e)    the term "business" includes the performance of professional services and of other activities of an independent character;

    f)    the term "international traffic" means any transport by a ship or aircraft, except when such transport is solely between places in a Contracting State;

    g)    the term "competent authority" means:

        i)    in Belgium: the Minister of Finance or his authorized representative; and

ii)      in the United States: the Secretary of the Treasury or his delegate;

h)      the term "Belgium" means the Kingdom of Belgium; when used in a geographical sense, such term means the territory of Belgium and includes the territorial sea and the seabed and subsoil and the superjacent waters of the adjacent submarine areas beyond the territorial sea over which Belgium exercises sovereign rights in accordance with international law;

i)      the term "United States" means the United States of America, and includes the states thereof and the District of Columbia; such term also includes the territorial sea thereof and the sea bed and subsoil of the submarine areas adjacent to that territorial sea, over which the United States exercises sovereign rights in accordance with international law; the term, however, does not include Puerto Rico, the Virgin Islands, Guam or any other United States possession or territory;

j)      the term "national" of a Contracting State means:

      i)      any individual possessing the nationality or citizenship of that State; and

      ii)      any legal person, partnership or association deriving its status as such from the laws in force in that State;

k)      the term "pension fund" means any person established in a Contracting State that is:

      i)      operated principally:

            A)      to administer or provide pension or retirement benefits; or

            B)      to earn income for the benefit of one or more arrangements described in A); and

      ii)      is either:

            A)      in the case of Belgium, an entity organized under Belgian law and regulated by the Bank Finance and Insurance Commission; or

            B)      in the case of the United States, exempt from tax in the United States with respect to the activities described in clause i) of this subparagraph.

2.    As regards the application of the Convention at any time by a Contracting State, any term not defined therein shall, unless the context otherwise requires, or the competent authorities agree to a common meaning pursuant to the provisions of Article 24 (Mutual Agreement Procedure), have the meaning which it has at that time under the law of that State for the purposes of the taxes to which the Convention applies, any meaning under the applicable tax laws of that State prevailing over a meaning given to the term under other laws of that State.

## Article 4
### RESIDENT

1.    For the purposes of this Convention, the term "resident of a Contracting State" means any person who, under the laws of that State, is liable to tax therein by reason of his domicile, residence, citizenship, place of management, place of incorporation, or any other criterion of a similar nature, and also includes that State and any political subdivision or local authority thereof. This term, however, does not include any person who is liable to tax in that State in respect only of income from sources in that State or of profits attributable to a permanent establishment in that State.

2.    An individual who is a United States citizen or an alien admitted to the United States for permanent residence (a "green card" holder) is a resident of the United States only if the individual has a substantial presence, permanent home or habitual abode in the United States and if that individual is not a resident of a State other than Belgium for the purposes of a double taxation convention between that State and Belgium.

3.    The term "resident of a Contracting State" includes:

a)    a pension fund established in that State; and

b)    an organization that is established and maintained in that State exclusively for religious, charitable, scientific, artistic, cultural, or educational purposes,

notwithstanding that all or part of its income or gains may be exempt from tax under the domestic law of that State.

4.    Where, by reason of the provisions of paragraph 1, an individual is a resident of both Contracting States, then his status shall be determined as follows:

a) he shall be deemed to be a resident only of the State in which he has a permanent home available to him; if he has a permanent home available to him in both States, he shall be deemed to be a resident only of the State with which his personal and economic relations are closer (center of vital interests);

b) if the State in which he has his center of vital interests cannot be determined, or if he does not have a permanent home available to him in either State, he shall be deemed to be a resident only of the State in which he has an habitual abode;

c) if he has an habitual abode in both States or in neither of them, he shall be deemed to be a resident only of the State of which he is a national;

d) if he is a national of both States or of neither of them, the competent authorities of the Contracting States shall endeavor to settle the question by mutual agreement.

5. Where by reason of the provisions of paragraph 1 a person other than an individual is a resident of both Contracting States, the competent authorities of the Contracting States shall by mutual agreement procedure endeavor to settle the question. If the competent authorities do not reach such an agreement, that person shall not be entitled to claim any benefit provided by the Convention, except those provided by paragraph 1 of Article 22 (Relief from Double Taxation), by paragraph 1 of Article 23 (Non-Discrimination) and by Article 24 (Mutual Agreement Procedure).

### Article 5

### PERMANENT ESTABLISHMENT

1. For the purposes of this Convention, the term "permanent establishment" means a fixed place of business through which the business of an enterprise is wholly or partly carried on.

2. The term "permanent establishment" includes especially:

a) a place of management;

b) a branch;

c) an office;

d) a factory;

e) a workshop; and

f)      a mine, an oil or gas well, a quarry, or any other place of extraction of natural resources.

3.     a)      A building site or construction or installation project constitutes a permanent establishment only if it lasts for more than twelve months.

      b)      An installation used for the exploration for natural resources constitutes a permanent establishment in a Contracting State only if it lasts or the activity continues in that State for more than twelve months.

4.     Notwithstanding the preceding provisions of this Article, the term "permanent establishment" shall be deemed not to include:

      a)      the use of facilities solely for the purpose of storage, display or delivery of goods or merchandise belonging to the enterprise;

      b)      the maintenance of a stock of goods or merchandise belonging to the enterprise solely for the purpose of storage, display or delivery;

      c)      the maintenance of a stock of goods or merchandise belonging to the enterprise solely for the purpose of processing by another enterprise;

      d)      the maintenance of a fixed place of business solely for the purpose of purchasing goods or merchandise, or of collecting information, for the enterprise;

      e)      the maintenance of a fixed place of business solely for the purpose of carrying on, for the enterprise, any other activity of a preparatory or auxiliary character;

      f)      the maintenance of a fixed place of business solely for any combination of the activities mentioned in subparagraphs a) through e), provided that the overall activity of the fixed place of business resulting from this combination is of a preparatory or auxiliary character.

5.     Notwithstanding the provisions of paragraphs 1 and 2, where a person -- other than an agent of an independent status to whom paragraph 6 applies -- is acting on behalf of an enterprise and has and habitually exercises in a Contracting State an authority to conclude contracts that are binding on the enterprise, that enterprise shall be deemed to have a permanent establishment in that State in respect of any activities that the person undertakes for the enterprise, unless the activities of such person are limited to those mentioned in paragraph 4

that, if exercised through a fixed place of business, would not make this fixed place of business a permanent establishment under the provisions of that paragraph.

6. An enterprise shall not be deemed to have a permanent establishment in a Contracting State merely because it carries on business in that State through a broker, general commission agent, or any other agent of an independent status, provided that such persons are acting in the ordinary course of their business as independent agents.

7. The fact that a company that is a resident of a Contracting State controls or is controlled by a company that is a resident of the other Contracting State, or that carries on business in that other State (whether through a permanent establishment or otherwise), shall not be taken into account in determining whether either company has a permanent establishment in that other State.

## Article 6

### INCOME FROM REAL PROPERTY

1. Income derived by a resident of a Contracting State from real property, including income from agriculture or forestry, situated in the other Contracting State may be taxed in that other State.

2. The term "real property" shall have the meaning which it has under the law of the Contracting State in which the property in question is situated. The term shall in any case include property accessory to real property (including livestock and equipment used in agriculture and forestry), rights to which the provisions of general law respecting landed property apply, usufruct of real property and rights to variable or fixed payments as consideration for the working of, or the right to work, mineral deposits, sources and other natural resources. Ships and aircraft shall not be regarded as real property.

3. The provisions of paragraph 1 shall apply to income derived from the direct use, letting, or use in any other form of real property.

4. The provisions of paragraphs 1 and 3 shall also apply to the income from real property of an enterprise.

5.      A resident of a Contracting State who is liable to tax in the other Contracting State on income from real property situated in the other Contracting State may elect for any taxable year to compute the tax on such income on a net basis as if such income were business profits attributable to a permanent establishment in such other State.  Any such election shall be binding for the taxable year of the election and all subsequent taxable years unless the competent authority of the Contracting State in which the property is situated agrees to terminate the election.

## Article 7

### BUSINESS PROFITS

1.      The profits of an enterprise of a Contracting State shall be taxable only in that State unless the enterprise carries on business in the other Contracting State through a permanent establishment situated therein.  If the enterprise carries on business as aforesaid, the profits of the enterprise may be taxed in the other State but only so much of them as are attributable to that permanent establishment.

2.      Subject to the provisions of paragraph 3, where an enterprise of a Contracting State carries on business in the other Contracting State through a permanent establishment situated therein, there shall in each Contracting State be attributed to that permanent establishment the profits that it might be expected to make if it were a distinct and independent enterprise engaged in the same or similar activities under the same or similar conditions.

3.      In determining the profits of a permanent establishment, there shall be allowed as deductions expenses that are incurred for the purposes of the permanent establishment, including executive and general administrative expenses so incurred, whether in the State in which the permanent establishment is situated or elsewhere.

4.      No profits shall be attributed to a permanent establishment by reason of the mere purchase by that permanent establishment of goods or merchandise for the enterprise.

5.      For the purposes of the preceding paragraphs, the profits to be attributed to the permanent establishment shall be determined by the same method year by year unless there is good and sufficient reason to the contrary.

6.      Where profits include items of income that are dealt with separately in other Articles of the Convention, then the provisions of those Articles shall not be affected by the provisions of this Article.

7.      In applying this Article, paragraph 8 of Article 10 (Dividends), paragraph 4 of Article 11 (Interest), paragraph 3 of Article 12 (Royalties), paragraph 3 of Article 13 (Gains) and paragraph 2 of Article 20 (Other Income), any income or gain attributable to a permanent establishment during its existence is taxable in the Contracting State where such permanent establishment is situated even if the payments are deferred until such permanent establishment has ceased to exist.

## Article 8

### SHIPPING AND AIR TRANSPORT

1.      Profits of an enterprise of a Contracting State from the operation of ships or aircraft in international traffic shall be taxable only in that State.

2.      For purposes of this Article, profits from the operation of ships or aircraft include, but are not limited to:

      a)      profits from the rental of ships or aircraft on a full (time or voyage) basis;

      b)      profits from the rental on a bareboat basis of ships or aircraft if the rental income is incidental to profits from the operation of ships or aircraft in international traffic; and

      c)      profits from the rental on a bareboat basis of ships or aircraft if such ships or aircraft are operated in international traffic by the lessee.

Profits derived by an enterprise from the inland transport of property or passengers within either Contracting State shall be treated as profits from the operation of ships or aircraft in international traffic if such transport is undertaken as part of international traffic.

3.      Profits of an enterprise of a Contracting State from the use, maintenance, or rental of containers (including trailers, barges, and related equipment for the transport of containers) shall be taxable only in that Contracting State, except to the extent that those containers or trailers and related equipment are used for transport solely between places within the other Contracting State.

4.      The provisions of paragraphs 1 and 3 shall also apply to profits from participation in a pool, a joint business, or an international operating agency.

## Article 9
### ASSOCIATED ENTERPRISES

1.      Where:

a)      an enterprise of a Contracting State participates directly or indirectly in the management, control or capital of an enterprise of the other Contracting State; or

b)      the same persons participate directly or indirectly in the management, control, or capital of an enterprise of a Contracting State and an enterprise of the other Contracting State,

and in either case conditions are made or imposed between the two enterprises in their commercial or financial relations that differ from those that would be made between independent enterprises, then, any profits that, but for those conditions, would have accrued to one of the enterprises, but by reason of those conditions have not so accrued, may be included in the profits of that enterprise and taxed accordingly.

2.      Where a Contracting State includes in the profits of an enterprise of that State, and taxes accordingly, profits on which an enterprise of the other Contracting State has been charged to tax in that other State, and the other Contracting State agrees that the profits so included are profits that would have accrued to the enterprise of the first-mentioned State if the conditions made between the two enterprises had been those that would have been made between independent enterprises, then that other State shall make an appropriate adjustment to the amount of the tax charged therein on those profits.  In determining such adjustment, due regard shall be had to the other provisions of this Convention and the competent authorities of the Contracting States shall if necessary consult each other.

## Article 10

## DIVIDENDS

1.      Dividends paid by a company that is a resident of a Contracting State to a resident of the other Contracting State may be taxed in that other State.

2.      However, such dividends may also be taxed in the Contracting State of which the company paying the dividends is a resident and according to the laws of that State, but if the dividends are beneficially owned by a resident of the other Contracting State, except as otherwise provided, the tax so charged shall not exceed:

a)      5 percent of the gross amount of the dividends if the beneficial owner is a company that owns directly at least 10 percent of the voting stock of the company paying the dividends;

b)      15 percent of the gross amount of the dividends in all other cases.

3.      Notwithstanding the provisions of paragraph 2, where the company paying the dividends is a resident of the United States, such dividends shall not be taxed in the United States if the beneficial owner is:

a)      a company that is a resident of Belgium that has owned directly or indirectly shares representing 80 percent or more of the voting power in the company paying the dividends for a 12-month period ending on the date on which entitlement to the dividend is determined and:

i)      satisfies the conditions of clause i) or ii) of subparagraph c) of paragraph 2 of Article 21 (Limitation on Benefits);

ii)      satisfies the conditions of clauses i) and ii) of subparagraph e) of paragraph 2 of Article 21, provided that the company satisfies the conditions described in paragraph 4 of that Article with respect to the dividends;

iii)      is entitled to benefits with respect to the dividends under paragraph 3 of Article 21; or

iv)      has received a determination pursuant to paragraph 7 of Article 21 with respect to this paragraph; or

b)      a pension fund that is a resident of Belgium, provided that such dividends are not derived from the carrying on of a business by the pension fund or through an associated enterprise.

4.      Notwithstanding the provisions of paragraph 2, where the company paying the dividends is a resident of Belgium, such dividends shall not be taxed in Belgium if the beneficial owner of the dividends is:

a)      a company that is a resident of the United States that has owned directly shares representing at least 10 percent of the capital of the company paying the dividends for a 12-month period ending on the date the dividend is declared; or

b)      a pension fund that is a resident of the United States, provided that such dividends are not derived from the carrying on of a business by the pension fund or through an associated enterprise.

5.      Paragraphs 2, 3 and 4 shall not affect the taxation of the company in respect of the profits out of which the dividends are paid.

6.      a)      Subparagraph a) of paragraph 2 and subparagraph a) of paragraph 3 shall not apply in the case of dividends paid by a U.S. Regulated Investment Company (RIC) or a U.S. Real Estate Investment Trust (REIT). In the case of dividends paid by a RIC, subparagraph b) of paragraph 2 and subparagraph b) of paragraph 3 shall apply. In the case of dividends paid by a REIT, subparagraph b) of paragraph 2 and subparagraph b) of paragraph 3 shall apply only if:

i)      the beneficial owner of the dividends is an individual or a pension fund, in either case holding an interest of not more than 10 percent in the REIT;

ii)      the dividends are paid with respect to a class of stock that is publicly traded and the beneficial owner of the dividends is a person holding an interest of not more than 5 percent of any class of the REIT's stock; or

iii)      the beneficial owner of the dividends is a person holding an interest of not more than 10 percent in the REIT and the REIT is diversified.

b)      For purposes of this paragraph, a REIT shall be "diversified" if the value of no single interest in real property exceeds 10 percent of its total interests in real property. For the purposes of this rule, foreclosure property shall not be considered an interest in real property. Where a REIT holds an interest in a partnership, it shall be treated as owning directly a proportion of the partnership's interests in real property corresponding to its interest in the partnership.

7.      For purposes of this Article, the term "dividends" means income from shares or other rights, not being debt-claims, participating in profits, as well as income that is subjected to the same taxation treatment as income from shares under the laws of the State of which the payer is a resident.

8.      The provisions of paragraphs 1 through 6 shall not apply if the beneficial owner of the dividends, being a resident of a Contracting State, carries on business in the other Contracting State, of which the payer is a resident, through a permanent establishment situated therein, and the holding in respect of which the dividends are paid is effectively connected with such permanent establishment. In such case the provisions of Article 7 (Business Profits) shall apply.

9.      A Contracting State may not impose any tax on dividends paid by a resident of the other State, except insofar as the dividends are paid to a resident of the first-mentioned State or the dividends are attributable to a permanent establishment situated in the first-mentioned State, nor may it impose tax on a corporation's undistributed profits, except as provided in paragraph 10, even if the dividends paid or the undistributed profits consist wholly or partly of profits or income arising in that State.

10.      a)      A company that is a resident of one of the States and that has a permanent establishment in the other State or that is subject to tax in the other State on a net basis on its income that may be taxed in the other State under Article 6 (Income from Real Property) or under paragraph 1 of Article 13 (Gains) may be subject in that other State to a tax in addition to the tax allowable under the other provisions of this Convention.

b)      Such tax, however, may be imposed on only the portion of the business profits of the company attributable to the permanent establishment and the portion of the income referred to in the preceding sentence that is subject to tax under Article 6 or under paragraph 1 of Article 13 that, in the case of the United States, represent the dividend equivalent amount of such profits or income and, in the case of Belgium, is an amount that is analogous to the dividend equivalent amount.

11. The tax referred to in subparagraphs a) and b) of paragraph 10 shall not be imposed at a rate exceeding the rate specified in subparagraph a) of paragraph 2. In any case, it shall not be imposed on a company that:

    a)    satisfies the conditions of clause i) or ii) of subparagraph c) of paragraph 2 of Article 21 (Limitation on Benefits);

    b)    satisfies the conditions of clauses i) and ii) of subparagraph e) of paragraph 2 of Article 21, provided that the company satisfies the conditions described in paragraph 4 of that Article with respect to an item of income, profit, or gain described in paragraph 10;

    c)    is entitled under paragraph 3 of Article 21 to benefits with respect to an item of income, profit, or gain described in paragraph 10; or

    d)    has received a determination pursuant to paragraph 7 of Article 21 with respect to this paragraph.

12.    a)    Notwithstanding Article 29 (Termination):

        i)    paragraph 3 of this Article shall terminate on, and shall cease to be effective for amounts paid or credited on or after, January 1 of the 6th year following the year in which the Convention enters into force, unless, by June 30 of the 5th year following entry into force, the United States Secretary of the Treasury, on the basis of a report of the Commissioner of Internal Revenue, certifies to the Senate of the United States that Belgium has satisfactorily complied with its obligations under Article 25 (Exchange of Information and Administrative Assistance); and

        ii)    the United States may terminate paragraph 3 of this Article by giving written notice of termination to Belgium, through the diplomatic channel, on or before June 30 in any year. In such case, paragraph 3 hereof shall cease to be effective for amounts paid or credited on or after January 1 of the year next following that in which such notice is given. The United States will not give such notice of termination unless it has determined that Belgium's actions with respect to Articles 24 (Mutual Agreement Procedure) and 25 have materially altered the balance of benefits of the Convention.

b)    The competent authorities shall consult at least annually regarding any issues that arise with respect to the functioning of Articles 24 and 25 that otherwise might trigger a termination under subparagraph a).

## Article 11

### INTEREST

1.    Interest arising in a Contracting State and beneficially owned by a resident of the other Contracting State shall be taxable only in that other State.

2.    Notwithstanding the provisions of paragraph 1:

a)    interest arising in the United States that is contingent interest of a type that does not qualify as portfolio interest under United States law may be taxed by the United States but, if the beneficial owner of the interest is a resident of Belgium, the interest may be taxed at a rate not exceeding 15 percent of the gross amount of the interest;

b)    interest arising in Belgium that is determined with reference to receipts, sales, income, profits or other cash flow of the debtor or a related person, to any change in the value of any property of the debtor or a related person or to any dividend, partnership distribution or similar payment made by the debtor to a related person may be taxed in Belgium, and according to the laws of Belgium, but if the beneficial owner is a resident of the United States, the interest may be taxed at a rate not exceeding 15 percent of the gross amount of the interest; and

c)    interest that is an excess inclusion with respect to a residual interest in a real estate mortgage investment conduit may be taxed by each State in accordance with its domestic law.

3. The term "interest" as used in this Article means income from debt-claims of every kind, whether or not secured by mortgage, and whether or not carrying a right to participate in the debtor's profits, and in particular, income from government securities and income from bonds or debentures, including premiums or prizes attaching to such securities, bonds or debentures, and all other income that is subjected to the same taxation treatment as income from money lent by the taxation law of the Contracting State in which the income arises. Income dealt with in Article 10 (Dividends) and penalty charges for late payment shall not be regarded as interest for the purposes of this Convention.

4. The provisions of paragraph 1 shall not apply if the beneficial owner of the interest, being a resident of a Contracting State, carries on business in the other Contracting State, in which the interest arises, through a permanent establishment situated therein, and the debt-claim in respect of which the interest is paid is effectively connected with such permanent establishment. In such case the provisions of Article 7 (Business Profits) shall apply.

5. Interest shall be deemed to arise in a Contracting State when the payer is a resident of that State. Where, however, the person paying the interest, whether he is a resident of a Contracting State or not, has in a Contracting State a permanent establishment in connection with which the indebtedness on which the interest is paid was incurred, and such interest is borne by such permanent establishment, then such interest shall be deemed to arise in the State in which the permanent establishment is situated.

6. Where, by reason of a special relationship between the payer and the beneficial owner or between both of them and some other person, the amount of the interest, having regard to the debt-claim for which it is paid, exceeds the amount which would have been agreed upon by the payer and the beneficial owner in the absence of such relationship, the provisions of this Article shall apply only to the last-mentioned amount. In such case the excess part of the payments shall remain taxable according to the laws of each Contracting State, due regard being had to the other provisions of this Convention.

## Article 12

## ROYALTIES

1.      Royalties arising in a Contracting State and beneficially owned by a resident of the other Contracting State shall be taxable only in that other State.

2.      The term "royalties" as used in this Article means payments of any kind received as a consideration for the use of, or the right to use, any copyright of literary, artistic, or scientific work (including cinematographic films and software), any patent, trade mark, design or model, plan, secret formula or process, or for information concerning industrial, commercial or scientific experience.

3.      The provisions of paragraph 1 shall not apply if the beneficial owner of the royalties, being a resident of a Contracting State, carries on business in the other Contracting State through a permanent establishment situated therein and the right or property in respect of which the royalties are paid is effectively connected with such permanent establishment. In such case the provisions of Article 7 (Business Profits) shall apply.

4.      Where, by reason of a special relationship between the payer and the beneficial owner or between both of them and some other person, the amount of the royalties, having regard to the use, right, or information for which they are paid, exceeds the amount which would have been agreed upon by the payer and the beneficial owner in the absence of such relationship, the provisions of this Article shall apply only to the last-mentioned amount. In such case the excess part of the payments shall remain taxable according to the laws of each Contracting State, due regard being had to the other provisions of this Convention.

## Article 13

## GAINS

1.      Gains derived by a resident of a Contracting State that are attributable to the alienation of real property situated in the other Contracting State may be taxed in that other State.

2.      For the purposes of this Article the term "real property situated in the other Contracting State" shall include:

      a)      real property referred to in Article 6 (Income from Real Property); and

b)      where that other State is the United States, a United States real property interest.

3.      Gains from the alienation of movable property forming part of the business property of a permanent establishment that an enterprise of a Contracting State has in the other Contracting State, including such gains from the alienation of such a permanent establishment (alone or with the whole enterprise), may be taxed in that other State.

4.      Gains derived by an enterprise of a Contracting State from the alienation of ships or aircraft operated in international traffic or personal property pertaining to the operation of such ships or aircraft shall be taxable only in that State.

5.      Gains derived by an enterprise of a Contracting State from the alienation of containers (including trailers and related equipment for the transport of containers) used for the transport of goods or merchandise shall be taxable only in that State, unless those containers or trailers and related equipment are used for transport solely between places within the other Contracting State.

6.      Gains from the alienation of any property other than property referred to in paragraphs 1 through 5 shall be taxable only in the Contracting State of which the alienator is a resident.


**Article 14**

**INCOME FROM EMPLOYMENT**

1.      Subject to the provisions of Articles 15 (Directors' Fees), 17 (Pensions, Social Security, Annuities, Alimony, and Child Support), 18 (Government Service) and 19 (Students, Trainees, Teachers and Researchers), salaries, wages, and other similar remuneration derived by a resident of a Contracting State in respect of an employment shall be taxable only in that State unless the employment is exercised in the other Contracting State. If the employment is so exercised, such remuneration as is derived therefrom may be taxed in that other State.

2.      Notwithstanding the provisions of paragraph 1, remuneration derived by a resident of a Contracting State in respect of an employment exercised in the other Contracting State shall be taxable only in the first-mentioned State if:

a)      the recipient is present in the other State for a period or periods not exceeding in the aggregate 183 days in any twelve month period commencing or ending in the taxable year concerned; and

b)      the remuneration is paid by, or on behalf of, an employer who is not a resident of the other State; and

c)      the remuneration is not borne by a permanent establishment which the employer has in the other State.

3.      Notwithstanding the preceding provisions of this Article, remuneration described in paragraph 1 that is derived by a resident of a Contracting State in respect of an employment as a member of the regular complement of a ship or aircraft operated in international traffic shall be taxable only in that State.

### Article 15

### DIRECTORS' FEES

Directors' fees and other compensation derived by a resident of a Contracting State for services rendered in the other Contracting State in his capacity as a member of the board of directors of a company that is a resident of the other Contracting State may be taxed in that other Contracting State.

### Article 16

### ENTERTAINERS AND SPORTSMEN

1.      Income derived by a resident of a Contracting State as an entertainer, such as a theater, motion picture, radio, or television artiste, or a musician, or as a sportsman, from his personal activities as such exercised in the other Contracting State, which income would be exempt from tax in that other Contracting State under the provisions of Articles 7 (Business Profits) and 14 (Income from Employment) may be taxed in that other State, except where the amount of the gross receipts derived by such entertainer or sportsman, including expenses reimbursed to him or borne on his behalf, from such activities does not exceed twenty thousand United States dollars ($20,000) or its equivalent in euro for the taxable year of the payment.

2.    Where income in respect of personal activities exercised by an entertainer or a sportsman in his capacity as such accrues not to the entertainer or sportsman himself but to another person, that income may, notwithstanding the provisions of Articles 7 and 14, be taxed in the Contracting State in which the activities of the entertainer or sportsman are exercised, but only in cases in which the contract pursuant to which the personal activities are performed

    a)    designates (by name or description) the entertainer or sportsman; or

    b)    allows the other party to the contract (or some third person other than the entertainer, sportsman or the first-mentioned other person) to designate the individual who is to perform the personal activities.

### Article 17

### PENSIONS, SOCIAL SECURITY, ANNUITIES,
### ALIMONY, AND CHILD SUPPORT

1.    Subject to paragraph 2 of Article 18 (Government Service),

    a)    pensions and other similar remuneration beneficially owned by a resident of a Contracting State shall be taxable only in that State;

    b)    notwithstanding subparagraph a), the amount of any such pension or remuneration arising in a Contracting State that, when received, would be exempt from taxation in that State if the beneficial owner were a resident thereof shall be exempt from taxation in the Contracting State of which the beneficial owner is a resident.

2.    Notwithstanding the provisions of paragraph 1, payments made by a Contracting State under provisions of the social security or similar legislation of that State to a resident of the other Contracting State or to a citizen of the United States shall be taxable only in the first-mentioned State.

3.    Annuities derived and beneficially owned by an individual resident of a Contracting State shall be taxable only in that State. The term "annuities" as used in this paragraph means a stated sum paid periodically at stated times during a specified number of years, or for life, under an obligation to make the payments in return for adequate and full consideration (other than services rendered).

4. Alimony paid by a resident of a Contracting State to a resident of the other Contracting State shall be taxable only in that other State. The term "alimony" as used in this paragraph means periodic payments made pursuant to a written separation agreement or a decree of divorce, separate maintenance, or compulsory support, which payments are taxable to the recipient under the laws of the State of which he is a resident.

5. Periodic payments, not dealt with in paragraph 4, for the support of a child made pursuant to a written separation agreement or a decree of divorce, separate maintenance, or compulsory support, paid by a resident of a Contracting State to a resident of the other Contracting State, shall be taxable only in the first-mentioned State.

6. Income earned by a pension fund that is a resident of a Contracting State may be taxed as income of an individual who is a resident of the other Contracting State only when, and, subject to the provisions of paragraph 1 of this Article, to the extent that, it is paid to, or for the benefit of, that individual from the pension fund (and not transferred to another pension fund that is a resident of the first-mentioned Contracting State).

7. Where an individual who is a member or beneficiary of, or participant in, a pension fund that is a resident of one of the Contracting States (or in a similar fund that is a resident of a comparable third State) exercises an employment or self-employment in the other Contracting State:

a) contributions paid by or on behalf of that individual under a pension plan during the period that he exercises an employment or self-employment in the other Contracting State shall be deductible (or excludible) in computing his taxable income in that other Contracting State; and

b) any benefits accrued under the pension plan, or contributions made under the pension plan by or on behalf of the individual's employer, during that period shall not be treated as part of the employee's taxable income and any such contributions shall be allowed as a deduction in computing the taxable income of his employer in that other Contracting State.

The relief available under this paragraph shall not exceed the relief that would be allowed by the other Contracting State to residents of that Contracting State for contributions to, or benefits accrued under, a pension plan established in that Contracting State, in the case of the United States, or recognized for tax purposes in that Contracting State, in the case of Belgium.

8. The provisions of paragraph 7 of this Article shall not apply unless:

a) contributions by or on behalf of the individual, or by or on behalf of the individual's employer, under the pension plan (or under another similar pension plan for which the first-mentioned pension plan was substituted) were made before the individual began to exercise an employment or self-employment in the other Contracting State;

b) the individual has performed personal services in the other Contracting State for a cumulative period not exceeding ten calendar years; and

c) the competent authority of the other Contracting State has agreed that the pension plan generally corresponds to a pension plan recognized for tax purposes in that other Contracting State.

9. a) Where a citizen of the United States who is a resident of Belgium exercises an employment in Belgium the income from which is taxable in Belgium, the contribution is borne by an employer who is a resident of Belgium or by a permanent establishment situated in Belgium, and the individual is a member or beneficiary of, or participant in, a pension fund that is a resident of Belgium (or in a similar fund that is a resident of a comparable third State),

i) contributions paid by or on behalf of that individual under a pension plan during the period that he exercises the employment in Belgium, and that are attributable to the employment, shall be deductible (or excludible) in computing his taxable income in the United States; and

ii) any benefits accrued under the pension plan, or contributions made under the pension plan by or on behalf of the individual's employer, during that period, and that are attributable to the employment, shall not be treated as part of the employee's taxable income in computing his taxable income in the United States.

b) The relief available under this paragraph shall not exceed the lesser of:

i)      the relief that would be allowed by the United States to its residents for contributions to, or benefits accrued under, a generally corresponding pension plan recognized for tax purposes in the United States; and

ii)      the amount of the contributions or benefits that qualify for tax relief in Belgium.

c)      For purposes of determining an individual's eligibility to participate in and receive tax benefits with respect to a pension plan established in the United States, contributions made to, or benefits accrued under, a pension plan recognized for tax purposes in Belgium shall be treated as contributions or benefits under a generally corresponding pension plan established in the United States to the extent relief is available to the individual under this paragraph.

d)      This paragraph shall not apply unless the competent authority of the United States has agreed that the pension plan generally corresponds to a pension plan recognized for tax purposes in the United States.

10.    a)      For purposes of paragraphs 7 and 9, a similar fund that is a resident of a State other than a Contracting State will be considered to be a resident of a comparable third State only if that third State:

i)      is a member state of the European Union or any other European Economic Area state or any party to the North American Free Trade Agreement or Switzerland;

ii)      provides, under a tax treaty or otherwise, comparable favorable treatment for contributions to a pension fund that is a resident of the Contracting State that is providing benefits under paragraph 7 or 9; and

iii)      has an information exchange provision in a tax treaty or other arrangement with the Contracting State that is providing benefits under paragraph 7 or 9 that is satisfactory to that Contracting State;

b)      a pension plan is recognized for tax purposes in a Contracting State if contributions to the plan would qualify for tax relief in that Contracting State.

## Article 18

## GOVERNMENT SERVICE

1.  Notwithstanding the provisions of Articles 14 (Income from Employment), 15

(Directors' Fees), 16 (Entertainers and Sportsmen) and 19 (Students, Trainees, Teachers and

Researchers):

> a)  salaries, wages and other similar remuneration, other than a pension, paid to an
>
> individual in respect of services rendered to a Contracting State or a political
>
> subdivision or local authority thereof shall be taxable only in that State;
>
> b)  such remuneration, however, shall be taxable only in the other Contracting State
>
> if the services are rendered in that State and the individual is a resident of that State
>
> who:
>
> > i)  is a national of that State; or
> >
> > ii)  did not become a resident of that State solely for the purpose of rendering
> >
> > the services.

2.  a)  Notwithstanding the provisions of paragraph 1, any pension and other similar

> remuneration paid by, or out of funds created by, a Contracting State or a political
>
> subdivision or a local authority thereof to an individual in respect of services rendered
>
> to that State or subdivision or authority (other than a payment to which paragraph 2 of
>
> Article 17 (Pensions, Social Security, Annuities, Alimony, and Child Support) applies)
>
> shall be taxable only in that State;
>
> b)  such pensions and other similar remuneration, however, shall be taxable only in
>
> the other Contracting State if the individual is a resident of, and a national of, that State.

3.  The provisions of Articles 14, 15, 16 and 17 shall apply to salaries, wages, pensions,

and other similar remuneration, in respect of services rendered in connection with a business

carried on by a Contracting State or a political subdivision or a local authority thereof.

## Article 19

## STUDENTS, TRAINEES, TEACHERS AND RESEARCHERS

1.  a)  Payments, other than compensation for personal services, received by a student

or business trainee who is, or was immediately before visiting a Contracting State, a resident of the other Contracting State, and who is present in the first-mentioned State for the purpose of his full-time education or for his full-time training, shall not be taxed in that State, provided that such payments arise outside that State, and are for the purpose of his maintenance, education or training. The exemption from tax provided by this paragraph shall apply to a business trainee only for a period of time not exceeding two years from the date the business trainee first arrives in the first-mentioned Contracting State for the purpose of training.

b)      A student or business trainee within the meaning of subparagraph a) shall be exempt from tax in the Contracting State in which the individual is temporarily present with respect to income from personal services in an aggregate amount equal to $9,000 or its equivalent in euro annually. The competent authorities shall, every five years, adjust the amount provided in this subparagraph to the extent necessary to take into account changes in the U.S. personal exemption and standard deduction and the Belgian basic allowance (quotité exemptée/belastingvrije som).

c)      For purposes of this paragraph, a business trainee is an individual:

      i)      who is temporarily present in a Contracting State for the purpose of securing training required to qualify the individual to practice a profession or professional specialty; or

      ii)      who is temporarily present in a Contracting State as an employee of, or under contract with, a resident of the other Contracting State, for the primary purpose of acquiring technical, professional, or business experience from a person other than that resident of the other Contracting State (or a person related to such resident of the other Contracting State).

2.      An individual who is a resident of a Contracting State at the beginning of his visit to the other Contracting State and who is temporarily present in the other Contracting State for the purpose of teaching or carrying on research at a school, college, university or other educational or research institution shall be exempt from tax in the other Contracting State for a period not exceeding two years from the date of the individual's arrival in that other State on the

remuneration received in consideration of teaching or carrying on research. This paragraph shall not apply to income from research if such research is undertaken not in the public interest but primarily for the private benefit of a specific person or persons.

## Article 20

## OTHER INCOME

1.      Items of income beneficially owned by a resident of a Contracting State, wherever arising, not dealt with in the foregoing Articles of this Convention shall be taxable only in that State.

2.      The provisions of paragraph 1 shall not apply to income, other than income from real property as defined in paragraph 2 of Article 6 (Income from Real Property), if the beneficial owner of the income, being a resident of a Contracting State, carries on business in the other Contracting State through a permanent establishment situated therein and the income is attributable to such permanent establishment. In such case the provisions of Article 7 (Business Profits) shall apply.

## Article 21

## LIMITATION ON BENEFITS

1.      A resident of a Contracting State shall be entitled to benefits otherwise accorded to residents of a Contracting State by this Convention only to the extent provided in this Article.

2.      A resident of a Contracting State shall be entitled to all the benefits of this Convention if the resident is:

      a)      an individual;

      b)      a Contracting State or any political subdivision or local authority thereof;

      c)      a company, if:

            i)      its principal class of shares (and any disproportionate class of shares) is regularly traded on one or more recognized stock exchanges, and either:

                  A)      its principal class of shares is primarily traded on a recognized stock exchange located in the Contracting State of which the company is a resident (or, in the case of a company resident in Belgium, on a recognized stock exchange located within the European Union or in any other European Economic Area state, or, in the case of a company resident in the United States, on a recognized stock exchange located in another state that is a party to the North American Free Trade Agreement); or

B) the company's primary place of management and control is in the Contracting State of which it is a resident; or

ii) at least 50 percent of the aggregate voting power and value of the shares (and at least 50 percent of any disproportionate class of shares) in the company are owned directly or indirectly by five or fewer companies entitled to benefits under clause i) of this subparagraph, provided that, in the case of indirect ownership, each intermediate owner is a resident of either Contracting State;

d) a person described in paragraph 3 of Article 4 (Resident), provided that, in the case of a person described in subparagraph a) of that paragraph, either:

i) more than 50 percent of the person's beneficiaries, members or participants are individuals resident in either Contracting State; or

ii) the organization sponsoring such person is entitled to the benefits of this Convention pursuant to this Article; or

e) a person other than an individual, if:

i) on at least half the days of the taxable year at least 50 percent of each class of shares or other beneficial interests in the person is owned, directly or indirectly, by residents of the Contracting State of which that person is a resident that are entitled to the benefits of this Convention under subparagraph a), subparagraph b), clause i) of subparagraph c), or subparagraph d) of this paragraph; and

ii) less than 50 percent of the person's gross income for the taxable year, as determined in the person's State of residence, is paid or accrued, directly or indirectly, to persons who are not residents of either Contracting State entitled to the benefits of this Convention under subparagraph a), subparagraph b), clause i) of subparagraph c), or subparagraph d) of this paragraph in the form of payments that are deductible for purposes of the taxes covered by this Convention in the person's State of residence (but not including arm's length payments in the ordinary course of business for services or tangible property and payments in respect of financial obligations to a bank that is not related to the payor).

3. A company that is a resident of a Contracting State shall also be entitled to the benefits of the Convention if:

    a) at least 95 percent of the aggregate voting power and value of its shares (and at least 50 percent of any disproportionate class of shares) is owned, directly or indirectly, by seven or fewer persons that are equivalent beneficiaries; and

    b) less than 50 percent of the company's gross income, as determined in the company's State of residence, for the taxable year is paid or accrued, directly or indirectly, to persons who are not equivalent beneficiaries, in the form of payments (but not including arm's length payments in the ordinary course of business for services or tangible property and payments in respect of financial obligations to a bank that is not related to the payor), that are deductible for the purposes of the taxes covered by this Convention in the company's State of residence.

4.     a) A resident of a Contracting State will be entitled to benefits of the Convention with respect to an item of income derived from the other Contracting State, regardless of whether the resident is entitled to benefits under paragraph 2 or 3, if the resident is engaged in the active conduct of a trade or business in the first-mentioned State (other than the business of making or managing investments for the resident's own account, unless these activities are banking, insurance, or securities activities carried on by a bank, insurance company or registered securities dealer), and the income derived from the other Contracting State is derived in connection with, or is incidental to, that trade or business.

    b) If a resident of a Contracting State or any of its associated enterprises carries on a trade or business activity in the other Contracting State which gives rise to an item of income, subparagraph a) of this paragraph shall apply to such item only if the trade or business activity in the first-mentioned State is substantial in relation to the trade or business activity in the other State. Whether a trade or business activity is substantial for purposes of this paragraph will be determined based on all the facts and circumstances.

c) In determining whether a person is "engaged in the active conduct of a trade or business" in a Contracting State under subparagraph a) of this paragraph, activities conducted by persons connected to such person shall be deemed to be conducted by such person. A person shall be connected to another if one possesses at least 50 percent of the beneficial interest in the other (or, in the case of a company, at least 50 percent of the aggregate voting power and at least 50 percent of the aggregate value of the shares in the company or of the beneficial equity interest in the company) or another person possesses, directly or indirectly, at least 50 percent of the beneficial interest (or, in the case of a company, at least 50 percent of the aggregate voting power and at least 50 percent of the aggregate value of the shares in the company or of the beneficial equity interest in the company) in each person. In any case, a person shall be considered to be connected to another if, based on all the relevant facts and circumstances, one has control of the other or both are under the control of the same person or persons.

5. A person that is a resident of a Contracting State and functions as a headquarters company for a multinational corporate group shall also be entitled to all the benefits of this Convention otherwise accorded to residents of that Contracting State if that person satisfies any other specified conditions for the obtaining of such benefits. A person shall be considered a headquarters company for this purpose only if:

a) it provides a substantial portion of the overall supervision and administration of the group, which may include, but cannot be principally, group financing;

b) the corporate group consists of companies which are resident in, and engaged in an active business in, at least five countries, and the business activities carried on in each of the five countries (or five groupings of countries) generate at least 10 percent of the gross income of the group;

c)     the business activities carried on in any one country other than the State of residence of the headquarters company generate less than 50 percent of the gross income of the group;

d)     no more than 25 percent of its gross income is derived from the other State;

e)     it has, and exercises, independent discretionary authority to carry out the functions referred to in subparagraph a);

f)     it is subject to the same income taxation rules in its country of residence as persons described in paragraph 4; and

g)     the income derived in the other State either is derived in connection with, or is incidental to, the active business referred to in subparagraph b).

If the gross income requirements of subparagraphs b), c), or d) of this paragraph are not fulfilled, they will be deemed to be fulfilled if the required ratios are met when averaging the gross income of the preceding four years.

6.     Notwithstanding the preceding provisions of this Article, where an enterprise of Belgium derives interest, or royalties from the United States, and the income consisting of such interest, or royalties is exempt from taxation in Belgium because it is attributable to a permanent establishment which that enterprise has in a third state, the tax benefits that would otherwise apply under the other provisions of the Convention will not apply to such income if the tax that is actually paid with respect to such income in the third state is less than 60 percent of the tax that would have been payable in Belgium if the income were earned in Belgium by the enterprise and were not attributable to the permanent establishment in the third state. Any interest or royalties to which the provisions of this paragraph apply may be taxed in the United States at a rate that shall not exceed 15 percent of the gross amount thereof. The provisions of this paragraph shall not apply if:

a)     in the case of interest, as defined in Article 11 (Interest), the income from the United States is derived in connection with, or is incidental to, the active conduct of a trade or business carried on by the permanent establishment in the third state (other than the business of making, managing, or simply holding investments for the enterprise's own account, unless these activities are banking, or securities activities carried on by a bank, or registered securities dealer); or

b) in the case of royalties, as defined in Article 12 (Royalties), the royalties are received as compensation for the use of, or the right to use, intangible property produced or developed by the permanent establishment itself.

7. A resident of a Contracting State that is not entitled to benefits pursuant to the preceding paragraphs of this Article shall, nevertheless, be granted benefits of the Convention if the competent authority of the other Contracting State determines that the establishment, acquisition, or maintenance of such person and the conduct of its operations did not have as one of its principal purposes the obtaining of benefits under the Convention. The competent authority of the other Contracting State shall consult with the competent authority of the first-mentioned State before denying the benefits of the Convention under this paragraph.

8. For the purposes of this Article:

a) the term "principal class of shares" means the ordinary or common shares of the company, provided that such class of shares represents the majority of the voting power and value of the company. If no single class of ordinary or common shares represents the majority of the aggregate voting power and value of the company, the "principal class of shares" are those classes that in the aggregate represent a majority of the aggregate voting power and value of the company;

b) the term "disproportionate class of shares" means any class of shares of a company resident in a Contracting State that entitles the shareholder to disproportionately higher participation, through dividends, redemption payments, or otherwise, in the earnings generated in the other Contracting State by particular assets or activities of the company when compared to its participation in overall assets or activities of such company;

c) the term "shares" shall include depository receipts thereof;

d) the term "recognized stock exchange" means:

i) the NASDAQ System owned by the National Association of Securities Dealers, Inc. and any stock exchange registered with the U.S. Securities and Exchange Commission as a national securities exchange under the U.S.

Securities Exchange Act of 1934;

ii)     the Brussels Stock Exchange;

iii)    the Irish Stock Exchange and the stock exchanges of Amsterdam, Frankfurt, Hamburg, Lisbon, London, Madrid, Milan, Paris, Toronto and Zurich; and

iv)     any other stock exchanges agreed upon by the competent authorities of the Contracting States;

e)    a class of shares is considered to be regularly traded on one or more recognized stock exchanges in a taxable year if the aggregate number of shares of that class traded on such stock exchange or exchanges during the preceding taxable year is at least 6 percent of the average number of shares outstanding in that class during that preceding taxable year;

f)    a company's primary place of management and control will be in the Contracting State of which it is a resident only if executive officers and senior management employees exercise day-to-day responsibility for more of the strategic, financial, and operational policy decision making for the company (including its direct and indirect subsidiaries) in that State than in any other state, and the staffs conduct more of the day-to-day activities necessary for preparing and making those decisions in that State than in any other state;

g)    the term "equivalent beneficiary" means a resident of a member state of the European Union or of any other European Economic Area state or of a party to the North American Free Trade Agreement, or of Switzerland, but only if that resident:

i)    A)    would be entitled to all the benefits of a comprehensive tax convention between any member state of the European Union or any other European Economic Area state or any party to the North American Free Trade Agreement, or Switzerland, and the State from which the benefits of this Convention are claimed under provisions analogous to subparagraph a), subparagraph b), clause i) of subparagraph c) or subparagraph d) of paragraph 2, provided that if such convention does not contain a comprehensive limitation on benefits provision, the resident would be entitled to the benefits of this Convention by reason of subparagraph a), subparagraph b), clause i) of subparagraph c), or subparagraph d) of paragraph 2 if such person were a resident of one of the Contracting States under Article 4 (Resident); and

   B)   with respect to insurance premiums and to income referred to in Article 10 (Dividends), 11 (Interest), or 12 (Royalties), would be entitled under such convention to a rate of tax with respect to the item of income for which benefits are being claimed under this Convention that is at least as low as the rate applicable under this Convention; or

   ii)   is a resident of a Contracting State that is entitled to the benefits of this Convention by reason of subparagraph a), subparagraph b), clause i) of subparagraph c), or subparagraph d) of paragraph 2;

h)   with respect to dividends, interest, or royalties arising in Belgium and beneficially owned by a company that is a resident of the United States, a company that is a resident of a member state of the European Union will be treated as satisfying the requirements of subparagraph g) i) B) for purposes of determining whether such United States resident is entitled to the benefits of the Convention under this paragraph if a payment of dividends, interest, or royalties arising in Belgium and paid directly to such resident of a member state of the European Union would have been exempt from tax pursuant to any directive of the European Union, notwithstanding that the tax convention between Belgium and that other member state of the European Union would provide for a higher rate of tax with respect to such payment than the rate of tax applicable to such United States company under Article 10, 11, or 12.

## Article 22

### RELIEF FROM DOUBLE TAXATION

1.   In the case of Belgium, double taxation will be relieved as follows:

   a)   Where a resident of Belgium derives income, other than dividends, interest and royalties, which is taxed in the United States in accordance with the provisions of this Convention, Belgium shall exempt such income from tax but may, in calculating the amount of tax on the remainder of the income of that resident, apply the rate of tax which would have been applicable if such income had not been exempted.

b)      The exemption provided by subparagraph a) shall also be granted with respect to income treated as dividends under Belgian law, which is derived by a resident of Belgium from a participation in an entity that derives its status as such from the laws of the United States or any state thereof, where that entity has not been taxed as a corporation by the United States, provided that the resident of Belgium has been taxed by the United States, proportionally to his participation in such entity, on the income out of which the income treated as dividends under Belgian law is paid. The exempted income is the income received after deduction of the costs incurred in Belgium or elsewhere in relation to the management of the participation in the entity.

c)      Dividends derived by a company which is a resident of Belgium from a company which is a resident of the United States, shall be exempt from the corporate income tax in Belgium to the extent that exemption would have been accorded if the two companies had been residents of Belgium.

d)      Where dividends described in subparagraph c) are not exempted from the corporate income tax in Belgium, Belgium shall deduct from the corporate income tax relating to these dividends, the United States tax levied on these dividends in accordance with Article 10 (Dividends). This deduction shall not exceed that part of the corporate income tax which is proportionally relating to these dividends.

e)      Subject to the provisions of Belgian law regarding the deduction from Belgian tax of taxes paid abroad, where a resident of Belgium derives items of his aggregate income for Belgian tax purposes which are interest or royalties, the United States tax levied on that income shall be allowed as a credit against Belgian tax relating to such income.

f)      Where, in accordance with Belgian law, losses incurred by an enterprise carried on by a resident of Belgium in a permanent establishment situated in the United States, have been effectively deducted from the profits of that enterprise for its taxation in Belgium, the exemption provided for in subparagraph a) shall not apply in Belgium to the profits of other taxable periods attributable to that establishment to the extent that those profits have also been exempted from tax in the United States by reason of compensation for the said losses.

2.      In accordance with the provisions and subject to the limitations of the law of the United States (as it may be amended from time to time without changing the general principle hereof), the United States shall allow to a resident or citizen of the United States as a credit against the United States tax on income applicable to residents and citizens:

      a)      the income tax paid or accrued to Belgium by or on behalf of such resident or citizen; and

      b)      in the case of a United States company owning at least 10 percent of the voting stock of a company that is a resident of Belgium and from which the United States company receives dividends, the income tax paid or accrued to Belgium by or on behalf of the payer with respect to the profits out of which the dividends are paid.

For the purposes of this paragraph, the taxes referred to in paragraphs 3 a) and 4 of Article 2 (Taxes Covered) shall be considered income taxes.

3.      For the purposes of applying paragraph 2 of this Article, an item of gross income, as determined under the laws of the United States, derived by a resident of the United States that, under this Convention, may be taxed in Belgium shall be deemed to be income from sources in Belgium.

4.      Where a resident of Belgium is also a citizen or a former citizen or former long-term resident of the United States and is subject to United States tax in accordance with paragraph 4 of Article 1 (General Scope), the following rules shall apply:

      a)      taxation by the United States of the income of such persons shall not affect the taxation in Belgium of income from sources arising in third countries, as determined under the laws of Belgium, and received by a resident of Belgium;

      b)      in the case of income from sources within the United States, Belgium shall apply paragraph 1 as if the tax paid to the United States in respect of such income were the tax that would have been paid to the United States if the resident were not a citizen or a former citizen or a former long-term resident of the United States;

c)     for purposes of applying paragraph 2 to compute United States tax on those items of income referred to in subparagraph b), the United States shall allow as a credit against United States tax the income tax paid to Belgium in accordance with subparagraph b); the credit so allowed shall not reduce the amount of the United States tax below the amount that is taken into account in applying subparagraph b); and

d)     for the exclusive purpose of relieving double taxation in the United States under subparagraph c), items of income referred to in subparagraph b) shall be deemed to arise in Belgium to the extent necessary to avoid double taxation of such income under subparagraph c).

**Article 23**

**NON-DISCRIMINATION**

1.     Nationals of a Contracting State shall not be subjected in the other Contracting State to any taxation or any requirement connected therewith that is more burdensome than the taxation and connected requirements to which nationals of that other State in the same circumstances, in particular with respect to residence, are or may be subjected.  This provision shall also apply to persons who are not residents of one or both of the Contracting States.  However, for the purposes of United States taxation, United States nationals who are subject to tax on a worldwide basis are not in the same circumstances as nationals of Belgium who are not residents of the United States.

2.     The taxation on a permanent establishment that an enterprise of a Contracting State has in the other Contracting State shall not be less favorably levied in that other State than the taxation levied on enterprises of that other State carrying on the same activities.

3.     The provisions of paragraphs 1 and 2 shall not be construed as obliging a Contracting State to grant to residents of the other Contracting State any personal allowances, reliefs, and reductions for taxation purposes on account of civil status or family responsibilities that it grants to its own residents.

4.    Except where the provisions of paragraph 1 of Article 9 (Associated Enterprises), paragraph 6 of Article 11 (Interest), or paragraph 4 of Article 12 (Royalties) apply, interest, royalties, and other disbursements paid by a resident of a Contracting State to a resident of the other Contracting State shall, for the purpose of determining the taxable profits of the first-mentioned resident, be deductible under the same conditions as if they had been paid to a resident of the first-mentioned State.  Similarly, any debts of a resident of a Contracting State to a resident of the other Contracting State shall, for the purpose of determining the taxable capital of the first-mentioned resident, be deductible under the same conditions as if they had been contracted to a resident of the first-mentioned State.

5.    Enterprises of a Contracting State, the capital of which is wholly or partly owned or controlled, directly or indirectly, by one or more residents of the other Contracting State, shall not be subjected in the first-mentioned State to any taxation or any requirement connected therewith that is more burdensome than the taxation and connected requirements to which other similar enterprises of the first-mentioned State are or may be subjected.

6.    Nothing in this Article shall be construed as preventing either Contracting State from imposing a tax as described in paragraph 10 of Article 10 (Dividends).

7.    The provisions of this Article shall, notwithstanding the provisions of Article 2 (Taxes Covered), apply to taxes of every kind and description imposed by a Contracting State or a political subdivision or local authority thereof.


## Article 24

### MUTUAL AGREEMENT PROCEDURE

1.    Where a person considers that the actions of one or both of the Contracting States result or will result for such person in taxation not in accordance with the provisions of this Convention, it may, irrespective of the remedies provided by the domestic law of those States, and the time limits prescribed in such laws for presenting claims for refund, present its case to the competent authority of either Contracting State.  The case must be presented within three years from the first notification of the action resulting in taxation not in accordance with the provisions of the Convention.

2.      The competent authority shall endeavor, if the objection appears to it to be justified and if it is not itself able to arrive at a satisfactory solution, to resolve the case by mutual agreement with the competent authority of the other Contracting State, with a view to the avoidance of taxation which is not in accordance with the Convention.  Collection procedures shall be suspended during the period that any mutual agreement proceeding is pending.

3.      The competent authorities of the Contracting States shall endeavor to resolve by mutual agreement any difficulties or doubts arising as to the interpretation or application of the Convention.  In particular the competent authorities of the Contracting States may agree:

    a)      to the same attribution of income, deductions, credits, or allowances of an enterprise of a Contracting State to its permanent establishment situated in the other Contracting State;

    b)      to the same attribution of income, deductions, credits, or allowances between permanent establishments of an enterprise where the permanent establishments are located in the Contracting States, whether or not the enterprise is an enterprise of a Contracting State;

    c)      to the same allocation of income, deductions, credits, or allowances between persons;

    d)      to the settlement of conflicting application of the Convention, including conflicts regarding:

        i)      the characterization of particular items of income;

        ii)     the characterization of persons;

        iii)    the application of source rules with respect to particular items of income;

        iv)     the same meaning of any term used in the Convention;

    e)      to advance pricing arrangements; and

    f)      to the application of the provisions of domestic law regarding penalties, fines, and interest in a manner consistent with the purposes of the Convention.

4.      To the extent necessary to facilitate the resolution of a case that is the subject of a mutual agreement proceeding under the preceding paragraphs, the tax authorities of each Contracting State shall have the power to ask any person who may have relevant information

for the disclosure of such information and to conduct investigations and hearings notwithstanding any time limits in their domestic tax laws that would otherwise bar such requests for information. Any agreement reached under this Article shall be implemented notwithstanding any time limits or other procedural limitations in the domestic law of the Contracting States.

5.     The competent authorities of the Contracting States may agree on administrative measures necessary to carry out the provisions of the Convention and particularly on the documentation to be furnished by a resident of a Contracting State in order to support its claim for the exemptions or reductions of tax provided for in the Convention.

6.     The competent authorities of the Contracting States may communicate with each other directly, including through a joint commission, for the purpose of reaching an agreement in the sense of the preceding paragraphs.

7.     Where, pursuant to a mutual agreement procedure under this Article, the competent authorities have endeavored but are unable to reach a complete agreement in a case, the case shall be resolved through arbitration conducted in the manner prescribed by, and subject to, the requirements of paragraph 8 and any rules or procedures agreed upon by the Contracting States, if:

    a)     tax returns have been filed with at least one of the Contracting States with respect to the taxable years at issue in the case;

    b)     the case is not a particular case that the competent authorities agree, before the date on which arbitration proceedings would otherwise have begun, is not suitable for determination by arbitration; and

    c)     all concerned persons agree according to the provisions of subparagraph d) of paragraph 8.

8.     For the purposes of paragraph 7 and this paragraph, the following rules and definitions shall apply:

    a)     the term "concerned person" means the presenter of a case to a competent authority for consideration under this Article and all other persons, if any, whose tax liability to either Contracting State may be directly affected by a mutual agreement arising from that consideration;

b)    the "commencement date" for a case is the earliest date on which the information necessary to undertake substantive consideration for a mutual agreement has been received by both competent authorities;

c)    arbitration proceedings in a case shall begin on the later of:

i)    two years after the commencement date of that case, unless both competent authorities have previously agreed to a different date, and

ii)    the earliest date upon which the agreement required by subparagraph d) has been received by both competent authorities;

d)    the concerned person(s), and their authorized representatives or agents, must agree prior to the beginning of arbitration proceedings not to disclose to any other person any information received during the course of the arbitration proceeding from either Contracting State or the arbitration board, other than the determination of such board;

e)    unless any concerned person does not accept the determination of an arbitration board, the determination shall constitute a resolution by mutual agreement under this Article and shall be binding on both Contracting States with respect to that case; and

f)    for purposes of an arbitration proceeding under paragraph 7 and this paragraph, the members of the arbitration board and their staffs shall be considered "persons or authorities" to whom information may be disclosed under Article 25 (Exchange of Information and Administrative Assistance) of the Convention.


## Article 25

## EXCHANGE OF INFORMATION AND ADMINISTRATIVE ASSISTANCE

1.    The competent authorities of the Contracting States shall exchange such information as may be relevant for carrying out the provisions of this Convention or of the domestic laws of the Contracting States concerning the taxes covered by the Convention insofar as the taxation thereunder is not contrary to the Convention, including information relating to the assessment or collection of, the enforcement or prosecution in respect of, or the determination of appeals in

relation to, the taxes covered by the Convention. The exchange of information is not restricted by paragraph 1 of Article 1 (General Scope).

2.    Any information received under this Article by a Contracting State shall be treated as secret in the same manner as information obtained under the domestic laws of that State and shall be disclosed only to persons or authorities (including courts and administrative bodies) involved in the assessment, collection, or administration of, the enforcement or prosecution in respect of, or the determination of appeals in relation to, the taxes referred to above, or the oversight of the above. Such persons or authorities shall use the information only for such purposes. They may disclose the information in public court proceedings or in judicial decisions.

3.    In no case shall the provisions of the preceding paragraphs be construed so as to impose on a Contracting State the obligation:

   a)    to carry out administrative measures at variance with the laws and administrative practice of that or of the other Contracting State;

   b)    to supply information that is not obtainable under the laws or in the normal course of the administration of that or of the other Contracting State;

   c)    to supply information that would disclose any trade, business, industrial, commercial, or professional secret or trade process, or information the disclosure of which would be contrary to public policy (ordre public).

4.    If information is requested by a Contracting State in accordance with this Article, the other Contracting State shall use its information gathering measures to obtain the requested information, even though that other State may not need such information for its own purposes. The obligation contained in the preceding sentence is subject to the limitations of paragraph 3 but in no case shall such limitations be construed to permit a Contracting State to decline to supply information because it has no domestic interest in such information.

5.    In no case shall the provisions of paragraph 3 be construed to permit a Contracting State to decline to supply information requested by the other Contracting State because the information is held by a bank, other financial institution, nominee or person acting in an agency or a fiduciary capacity or because it relates to ownership interests in a person. In order to obtain

such information the tax administration of the requested Contracting State shall have the power to ask for the disclosure of information and to conduct investigations and hearings notwithstanding any contrary provisions in its domestic tax laws.

6.    Notwithstanding paragraph 3, in order to obtain information requested within the framework of this Article, the tax administration of the requested Contracting State shall have the power to ask for the disclosure of information and to conduct investigations and hearings outside any time limits required in its domestic tax laws.

7.    Penalties provided by the domestic laws of the requested State for a person failing to give information relevant for carrying out its domestic tax laws shall apply as if the obligation to give information provided in paragraphs 5 or 6 was an obligation provided in the domestic tax laws of the requested State.

8.    Where a person refuses to give information requested within the framework of this Article or fails to give such information within the time required by the tax administration of the requested State, the requested State may bring appropriate enforcement proceedings against such person.  Such enforcement proceedings include, but are not limited to, summary summons enforcement proceedings in the case of the United States and summary proceedings (procédure en référé/procedure in kortgeding) in the case of Belgium.  Such person may be compelled to give such information under pain of such civil or criminal penalties as may be available under the laws of the requested State.

9.    If specifically requested by the competent authority of a Contracting State, the competent authority of the other Contracting State shall provide information under this Article in the form of depositions of witnesses and authenticated copies of unedited original documents (including books, papers, statements, records, accounts, and writings).

10.    The requested State shall allow representatives of the requesting State to enter the requested State to interview individuals and examine books and records.  Such interview or examination shall take place under the conditions and within the limits agreed upon by the competent authorities of both Contracting States.

11.    The competent authorities of the Contracting States shall agree upon the mode of application of this Article, including agreement to ensure comparable levels of assistance to each of the Contracting States.

12.    If the United States terminates paragraph 3 of Article 10 (Dividends) in accordance with paragraph 12 of Article 10, Belgium's obligations pursuant to paragraph 5 shall cease as of the date that paragraph 3 of Article 10 is no longer effective.

## Article 26

### ASSISTANCE IN COLLECTION

1.    Each of the Contracting States shall endeavor to collect on behalf of the other Contracting State such taxes imposed by that other Contracting State as will ensure that any exemption or reduced rate of tax granted under this Convention by that other Contracting State shall not be enjoyed by persons not entitled to such benefits.

2.    In no case shall this Article be construed so as to impose upon a Contracting State the obligation to carry out administrative measures at variance with the regulations and practices of either Contracting State or which would be contrary to the first-mentioned Contracting State's sovereignty, security, or public policy.

## Article 27

### MEMBERS OF DIPLOMATIC MISSIONS AND CONSULAR POSTS

Nothing in this Convention shall affect the fiscal privileges of members of diplomatic missions or consular posts under the general rules of international law or under the provisions of special agreements.

## Article 28

### ENTRY INTO FORCE

1.    This Convention shall be subject to ratification in accordance with the applicable procedures of each Contracting State. Each Contracting State shall notify the other through the

diplomatic channel, accompanied by an instrument of ratification, when it has completed the required procedures.

2.    The Convention shall enter into force on the date on which the later of the notifications is received, and its provisions shall have effect:

    a)    in respect of taxes withheld at source, for amounts paid or credited on or after the first day of the second month next following the date on which the Convention enters into force;

    b)    in respect of other taxes, for taxable periods beginning on or after the first day of January next following the date on which the Convention enters into force.

3.    Subparagraph f) of paragraph 5 of Article 21 (Limitation on Benefits) shall not have effect until January 1, 2011.

4.    The Convention between the United States of America and the Kingdom of Belgium for the Avoidance of Double Taxation and the Prevention of Fiscal Evasion with Respect to Taxes on Income, signed at Brussels on July 9, 1970, as modified by a Supplementary Protocol (the "prior Convention"), shall, in relation to any tax, cease to have effect as of the date on which this Convention has effect with respect to such tax in accordance with paragraphs 2 and 6 of this Article.

5.    Notwithstanding the preceding paragraph, where any person entitled to benefits under the prior Convention would have been entitled to greater benefits thereunder than under this Convention, the prior Convention shall, at the election of such person, continue to have effect in its entirety with respect to such person for a twelve-month period from the date on which the provisions of this Convention would have effect under paragraph 2 of this Article.

6.    Notwithstanding paragraphs 2 and 5, the provisions of Article 25 (Exchange of Information and Administrative Assistance) shall have effect from the date of entry into force of the Convention, without regard to the taxable period to which the matter relates.

7.    Notwithstanding paragraph 2, paragraphs 7 and 8 of Article 24 (Mutual Agreement Procedure) shall have effect, with respect to, and without regard to the taxable period to which the particular case relates:

a)      cases that are under consideration by the competent authorities as of the date on which this Convention enters into force; and

b)      cases that come under such consideration after such time,

and the commencement date for a case described in subparagraph a) of this paragraph shall be the date on which this Convention enters into force.


### Article 29

### TERMINATION

This Convention shall remain in force until terminated by a Contracting State. Either Contracting State may terminate the Convention at any time after 5 years from the date on which this Convention enters into force by giving notice of termination to the other Contracting State through diplomatic channels. In such event, the Convention shall cease to have effect:

a)      in respect of taxes withheld at source, for amounts paid or credited after the expiration of the 6-month period beginning on the date on which notice of termination was given; and

b)      in respect of other taxes, for taxable periods beginning on or after the expiration of the 6-month period beginning on the date on which notice of termination was given.


IN WITNESS WHEREOF, the undersigned, being duly authorized thereto by their respective Governments, have signed this Convention.

DONE at Brussels, in duplicate, in the English language, this twenty-seventh day of November, 2006.


FOR THE GOVERNMENT OF                FOR THE GOVERNMENT OF
THE UNITED STATES OF AMERICA:        THE KINGDOM OF BELGIUM:

www.ingramcontent.com/pod-product-compliance
Lightning Source LLC
Chambersburg PA
CBHW080621290526
45790CB00007B/2871